Why We Listen to Sermons

CALVIN SHORTS

A series published by the Calvin College Press
Titles in the Calvin Shorts Series:

Why We Listen to Sermons

Scott Hoezee

CALVIN SHORTS

Grand Rapids, MI • calvin.edu/press

Published 2019 by the Calvin College Press
3201 Burton St. SE
Grand Rapids, MI 49546

Scripture quotations are from the Holy Bible, New International
Version®. NIV®. Copyright © 1973, 1978, 1984, 2011 by Biblica, Inc.™
Used by permission of Zondervan. All rights reserved worldwide.
www.zondervan.com. The "NIV" and "New International Version" are
trademarks registered in the United States Patent and Trademark Office
by Biblica, Inc.™

Publisher's Cataloging-in-Publication Data

Names: Hoezee, Scott, 1964–, author.
Title: Why we listen to sermons / Scott Hoezee.
Series: Calvin Shorts.
Description: Includes bibliographic references. | Grand Rapids, MI:
Calvin College Press, 2019.
Identifiers: ISBN 978-1-937555-34-4 (pbk.) | 978-1-937555-35-1 (ebook)
| LCCN 2018961337
Subjects: LCSH Preaching. | Prayer meetings. | Worship (Religious
education) | Public worship. | Preaching—History. | BISAC RELIGION /
Sermons / Christian | RELIGION / Christian Ministry / Preaching
Classification: LCC BV4211.3.H64 2019 | DDC 251—dc23

Cover design: Robert Alderink
Interior design and typeset: Katherine Lloyd, The DESK

Contents

Series Editor's Foreword

Midway along the journey of our life
I woke to find myself in some dark woods,
For I had wandered off from the straight path.

So begins *The Divine Comedy*, a classic meditation on the Christian life, written by Dante Alighieri in the fourteenth century.

Dante's three images—a journey, a dark forest, and a perplexed pilgrim—still feel familiar today, don't they?

We can readily imagine our own lives as a series of journeys: not just the big journey from birth to death, but also all the little trips from home to school, from school to job, from place to place, from old friends to new. In fact, we often feel we are simultaneously on multiple journeys that tug us in diverse and sometimes opposing directions. We recognize those dark woods from fairy tales and nightmares and the all-too-real conundrums that crowd our everyday lives. No wonder we frequently feel perplexed. We wake up shaking our heads, unsure if we know how to live wisely today or tomorrow or next week.

This series has in mind just such perplexed pilgrims. Each book invites you, the reader, to walk alongside experienced guides who will help you understand the contours of the road as well as the surrounding landscape. They will cut back the underbrush, untangle myths and misconceptions, and suggest ways to move forward.

And they will do it in books intended to be read in an evening or during a flight. Calvin Shorts are designed not just for perplexed pilgrims but also for busy ones. We live in a complex and changing world. We need nimble ways to acquire knowledge, skills, and wisdom. These books are one way to meet those needs.

John Calvin, after whom this series is named, recognized our pilgrim condition. "We are always on the road," he said, and although this road, this life, is full of perplexities, it is also "a gift of divine kindness which is not to be refused." Calvin Shorts takes as its starting point this claim that we are called to live well in a world that is both gift and challenge.

In *The Divine Comedy*, Dante's guide is Virgil, a wise but not omniscient mentor. So, too, the authors in the Calvin Shorts series don't pretend to know it all. They, like you and me, are pilgrims. And they invite us to walk with them as together we seek to live more faithfully in this world that belongs to God.

Susan M. Felch
Executive Editor
The Calvin College Press

Additional Resources

Additional online resources for *Why We Listen to Sermons* may be available at www.calvin.edu/press.

Additional information, references, and citations are included in the notes at the end of this book. Rather than using footnote numbers, the comments are keyed to phrases and page numbers.

***Why We Listen to Sermons* is underwritten by the Calvin Institute of Christian Worship.**

Acknowledgments

This book was written during a sabbatical I received from Calvin Theological Seminary in the fall of 2018. Thus, I want to thank President Jul Medenblik, Academic Dean Ronald Feenstra, and the seminary Board of Trustees for arranging and approving my time away from my usual duties. I also acknowledge and thank two fellow pastors who stepped in to take over some of my work while I was away: Rev. Leonard Vanderzee took over my web writing responsibilities, and Rev. David Beelen stepped in to cover a course I co-teach in the fall semester. Thanks to them both.

As always, my colleague at the Center for Excellence in Preaching, Mary Bardolph, kept all things running smoothly while I worked on this book. Mary has long read most everything I write for publication, and she did that again—chapter by chapter—as this book came together. I thank her most heartily for that support and for everything she does.

At the Calvin College Press, Editor Susan Felch was incredibly helpful every step along the way, making needed corrections and keen suggestions to make this a better book. Dale Williams was also helpful in getting a design for the book. I thank Susan and Dale and also the many proofreaders, copyeditors, page designers, and others who had a hand in this project.

My colleague Paul Scott Wilson of Emmanuel College in Toronto was good enough to read the entire manuscript and—as he always does—made some wonderful additions to the book. I thank Paul for that and for all he and my seminary colleague John Rottman have taught me about preaching and the teaching of preaching these last many years.

The Calvin Institute of Christian Worship and its leadership team of John Witvliet, Kristen Verhulst, and Kathy Smith were good enough to provide funding for this book to see the light of day. I thank them and all my many colleagues at CICW.

Finally and as always, my wife, Rosemary, is a constant source of support. She was a sounding board for thoughts and ideas I had on this project, and she has for over thirty years now herself been the kind of discerning evaluator of sermons—my own sermons mostly!—that I hope this book helps others in the church to become. For all of that, I am so very grateful to Rosemary and my entire family.

Why
Sermons?

Life is full of rituals, routines, and predictable patterns. If you go to the movies, you know that you will sit through a good many previews of coming attractions before you get to the movie you came to see. If you go to a baseball game, there is the seventh inning stretch when everyone stands and sings a song in the middle of an inning fairly late in the game. And if you attend a church service, you will sing hymns and hear a sermon. When you are well accustomed to these rituals and traditions, you rarely question them. But once in a while, it can be useful to step back and wonder why we do the things we do.

The great preacher and theologian Jonathan Edwards did that once. He took a step back from all that was familiar about worship in the church to ask why. Why do we sing our faith? Why not just speak it? Why do we have sermons based on the Bible? Why not just *read* Scripture instead of having someone *talk* about it? These are very fine questions.

After all, Christians believe the Bible is like no other book in history. Christians confess that all of Scripture is "God-breathed," or inspired, as Paul once wrote to Timothy (2 Timothy 3:16). Although God used human authors and their various skills, the thoughts they conveyed were finally God's own thoughts. The resulting book is

15

confessed by orthodox believers as infallible, as wholly reliable in all things it intends to teach. The truth about humanity, sin, our need for a Savior, and God's redemptive plan are all in the Bible. It is an amazing book. It is a holy book.

So why not just spend our time reading it? Why don't we establish reading rooms like the Christian Science religion but in our case go to such places to read and reread and read again only the Bible? Even when we gather for worship, why not just have endless recitations of Scripture? If everything we need to know is in there, why do we clutter up worship with human words *about* the Bible in the form of sermons? Aren't the words of the preacher vastly secondary to the Bible anyway? Could those human words actually get in the way of the Bible's own words?

Again, these are good questions we may not often ask or ponder. But since this is a book about preaching, we want to wonder about such questions. What's more, we will wonder about them from the perspective of those who listen to sermons. Although I hope my fellow preachers will read and appreciate this book, my main goal is to help all those who attend church to become better listeners. Why do we listen to sermons in the first place? For what should we be listening? If we ever were asked formally to evaluate a sermon, what categories are appropriate to use in such critiques? These are the kinds of questions we will wonder about.

FROM THE BEGINNING

As we begin, we can note an obvious fact of history: ever since the founding of the church on the day of Pentecost, preaching has been a standard part of almost all Christian worship services. (Actually, and as we will see in the next chapter, some sense of preaching is present throughout the entire Bible.) Traditions may vary on the nature or length of a sermon, but throughout two thousand years of church history, we cannot find an era when preaching did not exist.

What's more, if Pentecost itself is any indication, it would seem that the Holy Spirit has long chosen preaching as the Spirit's primary way to get the gospel across to the world, because once that Spirit was poured out on the apostles, the very first thing that happened was that the apostle Peter preached a significant sermon. That sermon is the first of more than two dozen sermons that form the backbone of the Book of Acts. Preaching, it seems, has been with the church since the get-go. It is how the Spirit works. As Paul wrote in Romans 10, people cannot believe in a Savior they have never heard about. But then, "How can they hear without someone preaching to them?" (v. 14b).

But why preaching? Granted, in the earliest days of the church, copies of the Bible were rare. Certainly, no one owned a personal copy as people do today. Just reading the Bible, therefore, was not an option for most. Still, others could have read Scripture in worship while everyone else just listened. But no, there have always been sermons based on the Bible.

What does the sermon add to worship services that mere recitations of the Bible might not accomplish? A first thing to notice is this: the Bible's role as the foundation and root of the sermon has always been paramount. If a given sermon is not clearly bound up with a given text from Scripture, most judge it to be less of a sermon and more of a speech or a lecture. In most church traditions, those who wish to become pastors need to demonstrate clearly that they know how to craft sermons that are deeply rooted in the Bible alone.

Precisely because the Bible is God's own revelation, no one can hear reliably from God in a sermon if that message does not stem straight from Scripture. In short, sermons do not hide or obscure Scripture but showcase it. (So if you attend a church where more weeks than not you wonder, "What did that sermon have to do with the Bible?" then you have cause to be a bit worried as to what your pastor is up to. We will talk about how to evaluate sermons, including whether or not they count as biblical, in chapter 3.)

Sermons showcase Scripture. Again, though, what do sermons accomplish that just reading the text would not? Simply put, the fact that the Spirit has always used sermons is itself a way to honor the Bible. Precisely because the Bible is God's own holy Word, we rightly assume it is deep and rich. Yes, we can learn a lot just reading the Bible. On one level, the Bible is simple, clear. But on another level, the Bible contains mysteries and truths so mind-boggling that we will never finish exhausting its riches. It has been said that the Bible is like a body of water. In one sense, it is shallow enough that a toddler can splash around safely in it. But in another sense, this body of water is so deep that an elephant could easily drown in it. The message of Scripture is so plain and simple that many have come to faith just by reading the Gospel of Mark. But that same message is so wonderfully dense that many lifetimes would not be enough to plumb all the depths of even just Mark's Gospel.

The sermon exists somewhere in between those two poles. All preachers should hope that the simple message of Jesus and his love comes through every sermon. It is said that the great German theologian Karl Barth was once asked what he thought is the summation of all theology. Barth had written thousands of pages in his multivolume magnum opus *The Church Dogmatics*. But in answer to that question, he replied simply, "Jesus loves me this I know, for the Bible tells me so." Preaching begins there too.

But preaching also looks to those great mysteries and depths of the Bible. There is much the average person—and the average preacher!—is not going to grasp on a first or a quick reading. Sermons seek to extend into those depths in order to strengthen and deepen the faith of those who listen to them. But not just faith in the sense of knowledge. Sermons also deepen people's faith in the sense of having proper awe of God and his works.

GROWING UP

One of the first heresies the early church had to deal with was called Gnosticism. This school of thought has many features, but a key idea in Gnosticism is that we are saved in large part by knowledge, by what we know, by gaining access to secret information. The church has long rejected this idea. We are saved by grace alone. We are saved by God's love in Jesus Christ. This does not mean, however, that what we know as Christians is unimportant. The Bible seems to assume that true believers both will want to expand their grasp of God's Word and will in fact do so as time goes on.

The apostle Paul talked about this several times in his first letter to the quarrelsome believers in Corinth. He often had to note that they were still like infants or little children in the faith. But even as Paul noted this, he also pointed to the goal of greater understanding. "Brothers and sisters, I could not address you as people who live by the Spirit but as people who are still worldly—mere infants in Christ. I gave you milk, not solid food, for you were not yet ready for it. Indeed, you are still not ready" (1 Corinthians 3:1–2). But Paul's point is that they should be getting ready to handle more than just milk.

Paul sounds a similar theme when writing to the Christians in Ephesus. "So Christ himself gave the apostles, the prophets, the evangelists, the pastors and teachers, to equip his people for works of service, so that the body of Christ may be built up until we all reach unity in the faith and in the knowledge of the Son of God and become mature, attaining to the whole measure of the fullness of Christ. Then we will no longer be infants, tossed back and forth by the waves, and blown here and there by every wind of teaching and by the cunning and craftiness of people in their deceitful scheming. Instead, speaking the truth in love, we will grow to become in every respect the mature body of him who is the head, that is, Christ" (Ephesians 4:11–15). Clearly, Paul saw the need for all of us to grow up, to mature in our discipleship and our understanding of Christ.

Most people in the church are not biblical scholars. They are not professional theologians. All people vary a bit in terms of their intellectual prowess, and no one has ever said that a person is a better Christian if he or she is just generally a smarter person. Still, growth in the knowledge of God is expected in the Bible and in the church. Sermons seek to assist in this process of maturity. At heart, every sermon should seek to proclaim the Good News (as we will think about in chapter 4). The simple but glorious messages of "Jesus saves!" and "The kingdom of God is at hand!" should never be far from the heartbeat of every sermon preached.

But then sermons go beyond those simple declarations too. Sermons provide spiritual milk for those who still need it but also spiritual meat for those ready for more adult fare. Sermons explain those passages that seem difficult in the Bible. But sermons also reveal the hidden depths of texts that seem simple but that connect to God's grander story in ways we might miss without the guidance of a good teacher.

A good sermon on the Samaritan woman at the well in John 4, for instance, will point out that when the woman says, "I know that Messiah is coming," Jesus replies (in the Greek of the text) by saying simply, "I Am" (vv. 25–26). As it turns out, this is the first of the many "I Am" sayings in John. It also turns out that when Jesus says, "I Am," he is making a connection to the majestic name of God first revealed to Moses at the burning bush in Exodus 3: "Tell them I Am sent you" (see v. 14). For those with eyes to see and ears to hear, Jesus is making a mighty claim for himself by making a connection to the great I Am of Israel's God. A believer might miss such rich biblical connections without a teacher-preacher to point them out. But once we see such connections, we rejoice again over the arc of God's grand narrative in the Bible.

WORD AND WORLD

One other thing that a sermon may accomplish that a simple recitation of the Bible might not do ties in with our individual journeys as disciples of Christ. As we will explore throughout this book, preaching at its best creates a bridge between the biblical world from long ago and far away and our present time and place and culture. The Bible's truths are timeless, but their application varies over time and from place to place. We may be able to study old, historic sermons from Augustine or Luther and find value in what we can learn about the preaching craft from those ancient messages. But what no preacher can do is simply go into the pulpit and just read one of those old sermons and expect it will bear fruit in the lives of listeners. The context into which sermons from five hundred or one thousand years ago were preached is not our present context. The struggles and questions of the people back then—which one hopes the preacher was trying to take into account—may not be anyone's particular struggles or questions now.

In preaching, then, the Holy Spirit takes God's enduring, unchanging Word and through the insights and skills of the preacher brings that Word into contact with the real lives of those sitting in church on any given Sunday. Again, this may happen now and then when someone is reading the Bible for devotions. Even in such a private reading of the Bible, the Spirit may spark a similar interaction between the Word and the world today. But at its best, preaching can accomplish this for the entire church, for that portion of the body of Christ that is Deliverance Church in Nairobi, Kenya, or Trinity Church in Jacksonville, Florida. Through preaching, the entire church is built up.

In answer to Jonathan Edwards's question "Why preach?" we can say, "Because in preaching, the Spirit of God is active and alive. The Spirit through the sermon generates faith, quickens the pulse of those who already believe, and reveals the presence of the kingdom of God in the world we inhabit today. We preach because the Bible is a source of unending delight, and it is the joy of all who believe to plumb its depths and mine its riches now and even into eternity!"

To understand the sermon as the work of the Spirit, we will turn next in chapter 2 to a brief history of preaching. Knowing where preaching came from will enhance our ability to savor preaching today. Then in chapter 3, we will consider some formal categories by which we can assess and evaluate the sermons we hear. Since the Bible is the core of every sermon, chapter 4 will look at how and why the Bible is a source of unending delight and surprise. In chapter 5, we will ponder the mysteries of preaching and how the Spirit of God is able to do things through sermons that very often even preachers themselves could not have guessed would happen. Finally and briefly, in chapter 6, we will take a look ahead at the future of preaching.

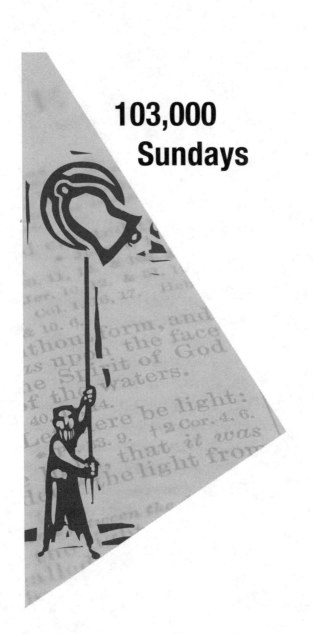

103,000
Sundays

2

S uppose we assume that the resurrection of Jesus from the dead happened around the year AD 30. If so, that counts as the very first Lord's Day. Jesus rose again the day after the Jewish Sabbath (a Saturday), and that is why the first day of the week, Sunday, became the official day of Christian celebration and worship. Since that time the world has seen just over 103,000 Sundays.

In the earliest days of the church, only a handful of sermons may have initially been preached each Sunday. Sermons were preached first in Judea and Samaria and then eventually in places like Corinth, Ephesus, Philippi, Galatia, and Rome. But as the number of churches multiplied worldwide, any given Sunday meant the preaching of more and more sermons. No one really knows—or has a reliable way to calculate—how many sermons have been preached in the last two thousand years. But common sense tells us it is a lot! By some estimates, there are approximately 3.4 million congregations worldwide now. If on average two sermons per week are preached in each church, that means each year roughly 354 million sermons are preached in the world.

There is a great deal of variation among those hundreds of millions of messages each year. Some are relatively short homilies lasting perhaps not much more than ten minutes. Others are far longer, lasting as long as forty-five minutes to an hour. The forms of these sermons vary too. Some are extemporaneous, off-the-cuff. Other sermons are delivered from carefully crafted manuscripts written by preachers who have given a great deal of advance thought to every verb and adjective in the message. Today some sermons are all words, whereas other sermons include visual aids, movie clips, music, or props of various kinds. Many sermons feature the voice of only the preacher, but some churches have explored more dialogic sermons that include live feedback from the congregation or the spoken testimonies of members of the church who are invited to share examples of God's work in their lives as part of the sermon.

But whatever their frequency, length, or form, sermons remain a staple of Christian worship services all over the world. How did this come about? What is the background in history for the spoken sermon? Before we explore the nuts and bolts of what makes sermons work, let's take a brief look at where preaching came from in the Judeo-Christian tradition.

As we dive into this history, you may wonder, "Why are we doing this?" It is a fair question. Simply put, seeing the history of preaching, especially the biblical roots of preaching, should bless us with the sense that we are part of a very long, living tradition. Preaching in its various forms has long been God's way to communicate with God's people. The more we understand the background of preaching, the better we can celebrate God's work today. When we listen to sermons, we are part of what

Hebrews 12:1 calls a "great cloud of witnesses." It is our privilege to take our place among those brothers and sisters throughout the ages. Exploring a little history, then, may generate some grateful joy in our hearts.

THE FIRST SERMON?

In chapter 1, I suggested that the very first sermon of the church came from the apostle Peter on the day of Pentecost. Pentecost is often called the birthday of the church, the first day when the Spirit was poured out in power. If so, then the fact that a sermon was the first big thing that happened that day tells us a great deal about the place of preaching in the life of the church from then on. Pentecost was the first time that the resurrection of Jesus Christ from the dead was publicly proclaimed as gospel—Good News. (Actually, the very first proclamation of the resurrection was made by the women who told the message of the angels to the other disciples.) But was Peter's message really the first time in the Bible we can see something like the modern sermon? The obvious answer is no, not least because Jesus preached many sermons. The Sermon on the Mount alone reminds us that, in a way, the disciples-turned-apostles were only doing what they had seen Jesus the Master do first.

But was even Jesus the first preacher? Again, the answer is no, because in the New Testament, we first encounter the preaching of John the Baptist. John's fiery sermons about the need to repent and be baptized paved the way for the arrival of God's Messiah in Jesus of Nazareth. But the fact that John was a preacher is significant for another very important reason. John the Baptist was not only the first New Testament era preacher but also the last in a long line of Old Testament prophets.

When God formed the descendants of Abraham and Sarah into the chosen nation of Israel, he established the office of priest. Priests, however, were not ministers or preachers in the way we understand those positions today. There was, however, in Israel a recognized formal office or calling that did serve as the forerunner to preachers later in history: the prophet. Moses is considered the first great prophet of the Lord. That is significant because this means there was a prophet in Israel even before Moses's brother Aaron became the first priest. What's more, God formally promised Israel that even after Moses, there would always be a prophet (or many prophets) in the midst of Israel. The key biblical text that tells us this is in Deuteronomy 18: "I will raise up for them a prophet like you [Moses] from among their fellow Israelites, and I will put my words in his mouth. He will tell them everything I command him. I myself will call to account anyone who does not listen to my words that the prophet speaks in my name" (vv. 18–19).

God was faithful to this promise. In time, Joshua took Moses's place. Eventually, we encounter figures such as

Deborah, Nathan, Elijah, Elisha, Huldah, Isaiah, Jeremiah, and Ezekiel. Then there are the twelve others who make up the Minor Prophets, such as Jonah, Obadiah, and Amos. These prophetic figures did indeed proclaim the Word of God to Israel. Unlike modern preachers, however, they did not do this by opening up the Bible and interpreting a given text. Instead, God revealed himself and his sacred Word directly to the prophets. Then they were charged by God to speak those words to Israel. We often think of prophets as people who foretell the future and make predictions about upcoming events. And sometimes the Old Testament prophets did that. Mostly, however, what they did was not foretell but *forth*tell. They conveyed God's words to God's people.

Sometimes such messages were ones of comfort and hope. At other times they were words of judgment. Sometimes God gave a prophet a very specific word for a specific person (think of the prophet Nathan confronting King David about his adultery with Bathsheba). Other times God revealed messages aimed at all of God's people to call them back to their vocation of living as God's holy people in an unholy world. Such prophets were not interpreting a given text the way a preacher may do today. But their words did hark back to the Torah, to God's revealed Law in the first five books of the Bible. In that sense, the prophets were like modern preachers bringing the Word of God to bear on people's lives.

THE TRADITION CONTINUES

When John the Baptist went into the wilderness preaching, "Repent, for the kingdom of heaven has come near"
(Matthew 3:2), he was continuing a long tradition among
God's people. Jesus's own sermons did this too. Our Lord
carefully presented the revealed Word of God to Israel and
showed—as only the incarnate Son of God could do—
what those words of Scripture really meant. As just noted,
in some ways, the very first proclamation of the resurrection—the heart of the gospel—was preached by the
women to the disciples. All four Gospels show that it was
the women who went to Jesus's tomb early Easter morning who first heard—and then were charged to go back to
the disciples and repeat—the Good News that Christ was
risen from the dead. And on the day of Pentecost, when
Peter, filled with the Spirit's power, stood up to declare,
"Fellow Jews and all of you who live in Jerusalem, let me
explain this to you; listen carefully to what I say" (Acts
2:14), he also was carrying on a tradition of proclaiming
God's Word that went back to Moses.

After Pentecost, preaching became a hallmark of the
apostles. As noted in the first chapter, the Book of Acts
is structured around twenty-seven sermons (or speeches
that were essentially sermons) preached by apostles such
as Peter, John, and Paul. Before the New Testament con-
cludes, we see the mantle of preaching being bestowed
on a younger generation of preachers such as Titus and
Timothy. The two letters to Timothy and the one to Titus

are called the Pastoral Epistles because they contain Paul's advice for Titus and Timothy on how best to pastor and to preach. A well-known passage addressed to Timothy has become something of the standard advice to all preachers since: "In the presence of God and of Christ Jesus, who will judge the living and the dead, and in view of his appearing and his kingdom, I give you this charge: Preach the word; be prepared in season and out of season; correct, rebuke and encourage—with great patience and careful instruction" (2 Timothy 4:1–2).

Preaching the Good News of the gospel continued from that time on. At first, preaching was often done in secret when the church was persecuted by Rome. But after Christianity became an accepted religion—if not the official religion of the Roman Empire—preaching very soon became more prominent, as did those who were skilled at the craft. Although they wrote many other pieces of theological reflection, the earliest so-called Church Fathers were best known for their sermons. Cyril of Jerusalem, Origen, Ambrose, Augustine, and others left behind many intricate (and sometimes by today's standards also really long) sermons. One early church preacher was so gifted at preaching that he acquired a name that reflected his eloquence in the pulpit: Chrysostom, whose name means "golden mouth."

This brief book is not the place to summarize two thousand years of preaching in Christ's church. Indeed, each church tradition has its own history: Anglican,

Methodist, Reformed, Baptist, Catholic, Orthodox, Pentecostal. But we can quickly note a few key developments.

The Middle Ages, for instance, saw a great deal of development in preaching, including now and again special permission being granted to women, such as Hildegard of Bingen, whose gifts of proclamation were put into service in the Roman Church. Two other key figures from the eleventh and twelfth centuries are Francis of Assisi and Dominic. Francis was known as a skilled preacher from an early age. (This is in part why the current pope, himself an outstanding preacher, took the name Francis.) Dominic is remembered for establishing the Dominican Order specifically as the Order of Preachers (OP), which continues today and recently celebrated its eight hundredth anniversary. Many scholars see the Order of Preachers as key to the development of the type of sermon that persists to this day. Instead of using a commentary-like, verse-by-verse explanation (typical of many sermons up to that time), Dominic and his Order of Preachers saw the sermon as its own literary form, with themes and imagery springing from a biblical text.

By the time of the Protestant Reformation in the sixteenth century, worship in general—and sometimes preaching as well—had become more mysterious to churchgoers in some parts of the world. This was due in no small part to the fact that worship was often conducted in Latin, which few people spoke or understood. When priests celebrated the Mass and said in Latin the words of

Jesus "This is my body," they said, "Hoc est corpus meum." Some claim that since few people understood those words, they sounded like "hocus pocus" to many people, thus possibly giving birth to that phrase used ever since to refer to something magically mysterious.

PREACHING REVITALIZED

When the Reformation came along, however, preaching in the newly established Protestant churches regained a high profile. The Reformation was, after all, premised on the idea that what the Scriptures actually taught was different from what the church had been promoting. Martin Luther's discovery of what Paul taught in the Letter to the Romans was revolutionary for his understanding of salvation by grace alone through faith alone apart from works. John Calvin and many other Reformers followed Luther's path. Thanks to the invention of the printing press, copies of the Bible, often in the language of the people (German, French, English, etc.), were more readily available to churches and individuals than had been true before. Since proclaiming what the Bible actually taught was the key to the Reformation, preaching became primary. People such as Luther and Calvin preached sermons not just on Sundays but *every day*, sometimes even more than once a day. John Calvin preached as many as 290 times per year.

Sermons in the language of the people spread the message of the gospel throughout the European churches and then beyond into the so-called New World of North America, Africa, and the Far East. As missionaries traveled to places such as Africa and Asia, they took with them the preaching traditions of their sending churches. They adapted their preaching to the cultural contexts, but the form of the preaching had clear ties to their home churches. (A few years ago when I was in Asia, I was surprised to see that to this day a great many Asian preachers in Protestant churches still deliver three-point sermons not unlike what many in the West grew up hearing.)

Meanwhile, Protestant catechisms sprang up across Europe in the sixteenth and seventeenth centuries. The church had long used catechism-like summaries as teaching tools. Even the earliest creeds, such as the Apostles' and Nicene Creeds, were mini-catechisms in a way. But with the rise of the newly formed Protestant churches and their distinctive interpretations of the Bible, catechisms proliferated. A catechism was designed to summarize the key teachings of the Bible in order to teach people more quickly the message of Scripture. Most such catechisms were written in a question-and-answer format. "What does it mean that Jesus ascended into heaven?" a catechism might ask before then answering the question biblically. In addition to well-known catechisms such as Luther's Shorter and Longer Catechisms and the Heidelberg Catechism, a multitude of local catechisms were composed to instruct the youth and people of all ages in the true doctrines of the Bible. Thus, catechetical preaching also grew in prominence. Preachers at times based their sermons less on a single biblical text and more on a part of a given catechism, bringing in multiple Bible texts to bolster doctrinal points.

In the centuries since the Reformation, certain eras saw major developments in the form of sermons. Puritan plain-style preaching laid emphasis on reason and logic. During the First Great Awakening in the eighteenth century, Jonathan Edwards, George Whitefield, and John Wesley engaged in powerful evangelistic preaching that appealed to people's feelings and experiences in an effort to convert them. (It is said that George Whitefield was so eloquent that he could make women faint and grown men weep just by how he pronounced the word *Mesopotamia*!) The Second Great Awakening in the nineteenth century included women preachers, both black and white, such as Sojourner Truth and Phoebe Palmer. Charles Finney and later fiery evangelists such as Billy Sunday continued a trend of appealing to people's emotions.

HEAD AND HEART

But while some nineteenth- and early twentieth-century preaching centered on emotional appeals, other preaching became a means of addressing social concerns. In England, Catherine Mumford Booth, who with her husband started the Salvation Army, became known for her preaching and ministry, meeting desperate social needs in the culture.

Preachers such as Washington Gladden and Walter Raus-
chenbusch founded the movement that became known as
the Social Gospel. They asserted that the church's truest
calling was to proclaim care for the poor and to address
social injustice. As psychology grew in importance, some
preachers, such as Harry Emerson Fosdick at Riverside
Church in New York City, began to work hard to minister
to people's pastoral needs from the pulpit. African American churches were the center of black culture and tended
to keep social justice and piety together, often in highly
artful and expressive preaching. But some other traditions
were wary of both emotionalism and a focus on social
issues. In an effort to counteract such emphases, preachers in some churches turned toward being a bit intellectual
with a heavy emphasis on educating people's theological
minds and sensibilities.

In terms of sermon format, the reigning model of
preaching well into the middle of the twentieth century
was deductive. Deductive sermons relied on a system-
atic teaching of various points (usually three points, as
it turned out!). In my own tradition and other similar
churches, preachers were once taught what was called the
"its" template for preaching. A preacher might announce
at the start of the sermon, "Today's theme is justification,
and it has three parts: *its* origin in God's eternal decree,
its fulfillment in Christ's sacrifice, and *its* forensic application to our hearts by grace. First, then, its . . ." I recently
ran across my late father-in-law's ordination sermon from

1951. His extended outline contained no fewer than nineteen points and subpoints, each of which began with "Its"!

This model began to change in the mid- to late-twentieth century, however. Although deductive and point-by-point preaching is by no means extinct, it has been largely eclipsed by an inductive model. Inductive sermons rely more on narrative and on an appeal to shared experiences between the preacher and the congregation. Doctrines may still be conveyed in sermons, but they are shown as coming out of biblical stories first of all. This change came about in part, as the preacher Fred Craddock noted in his landmark book *As One without Authority*, because after the 1960s and the questioning of traditional sources of authority, even preachers needed to gain people's respect by preaching sermons that were grounded in real-life experiences. Pastoral authority could no longer just be asserted. It had to be *earned*.

Stories have become more important. Demonstrating the real-world traction of Christian concepts and how this or that biblical text plays out in people's everyday lives are now hallmarks of many sermons. Instructing people's minds is still important, but so is an appeal to people's hearts. Perhaps there was a time when, to many churchgoers, the fact that a sermon was correct, orthodox, and true was enough. How or whether it applied to what someone might encounter on a Monday morning or a Thursday afternoon was less important than the fact that it proclaimed what was right.

Today, however, many people are far more interested in the question "So what?" Preaching at its best—as we thought about in chapter 1—has always been about bringing God's Word to bear on our lives today. For a long while, though, in some places, it was thought that perhaps a more intellectual, doctrinal application was enough. And there is value in knowing the truth clearly and well. But in the last half century, the emphasis of application has shifted to more practical, day-to-day concerns. How does this Bible passage help me navigate a world of doubt and cynicism? How might I be comforted by God's Word in a season of grief? How might this sermon help me reach out to someone who does not believe in Jesus whom I want to bring to the faith? Many preachers today are far more sensitive to questions like these than was true a century ago.

In some churches, this turn toward narrative and concrete application has become more prominent in the last half century. Yet African American preaching had long exhibited these very characteristics. As was the case with many well-known spirituals, this style of preaching emerged out of the pain of slavery. Sermons in this tradition emphasized biblical themes of hope and liberation with an eye fixed squarely on daily conditions of oppression. The sermons—often characterized by a call-and-response in which the congregation actively participated—ended with what is called celebration. The sermons climaxed with a joyful proclamation of hope that elicited great enthusiasm and joy from the congregation.

By way of example, think of the soaring conclusion to Martin Luther King Jr.'s speech (it was really a sermon) "I Have a Dream." King ended with celebration as he exuberantly quoted the words of the great spiritual: "Free at last, free at last, thank God Almighty, we are free at last!"

Only in recent years has this form of preaching been studied in a scholarly way by people such as Henry Mitchell and more recently Frank Thomas of Christian Theological Seminary. It deserves careful study, as it is clearly a unique style with roots in both African cultures and the experience of slavery. Indeed, this is a style of preaching in which application was in a way the whole point. In an interview I once heard, someone asked the renowned African American preacher James Cone why sermons in African American churches were so long. Cone replied by saying that six days a week black people are told they are of lesser—and maybe of no—value. Come Sunday, then, it just takes a while to talk them back into seeing who they really are: precious children of God. In a way, maybe that is a big part of what preaching was supposed to do all along.

Through the prophets from Moses forward, God wanted his people to know the truth. He wanted them to understand how to live in ways that would lead to delight and flourishing. Now Christians believe that all of God's Word and all of God's promises have found their final yes in Christ Jesus. Proclaiming this today continues to bring God's holy Word to God's people. We should hope and expect such preaching to be life-giving, to be a source of renewal and joy and a generator of hope. At its best throughout the ages, this is just what preaching has been.

But how do we evaluate how well a given sermon is accomplishing its task? We will turn to that vital question in the next chapter.

"How Was
the Sermon?"

3

When a baseball player connects with a pitch and sends the ball sailing over the back fence for a home run, we stand up and cheer. When an entrée at a restaurant wows us with its beautiful plating but more with its exquisite flavor, we send our compliments to the chef. When an orchestra plays the final note of a marvelous performance of a Mozart symphony, we applaud, perhaps even give a standing ovation. When we are on the receiving end of some kind of public offering—be it a sports game, a meal, or an arts performance—we have standard ways of reacting to show our appreciation. Of course, we also have some ways of responding if we need to signal disappointment. We might sit on our hands rather than applaud or cross our arms over our chests. We might boo. We might leave the restaurant and write a negative Trip-Advisor review.

Sermons are generally the most public thing the average pastor does in any given week. All of us who sit in the pews or on the folding chairs in whatever room constitutes a given congregation's worship space are on the receiving end of such preaching. Generally speaking, we all form opinions on sermons too. Often we share them only privately. On the way back from church or over Sunday noon dinner, the question "What did you think of the sermon?" is common. Sometimes, though, our responses are directed to the preacher himself or herself. In some traditions, there is what is known as call-and-response as members of the congregation routinely respond during the sermon by shouting out, "Amen!" or "Preach It!" or by clapping. In other traditions, there may often be comments at the church door. We shake the pastor's hand and perhaps say, "Nice sermon, pastor. I liked that. I was blessed by that. That was interesting." If we found the sermon to be less than inspiring, we may say nothing at all beyond "Nice to see you, pastor." Now and then we may venture a little farther into the territory of criticism: "That sermon seemed a little off to me for some reason, pastor."

All preachers like to hear "Good sermon." All preachers cringe to hear the opposite. Anyone who listens to a sermon is under no formal obligation one way or the other to provide sermon feedback every Sunday. But some who are in leadership—elders, deacons, or other staff members—are often charged with supervising the worship life of the church and so bear some responsibility to support the preacher by providing regular feedback on sermons. The problem most of us have, though, is that we often have no categories of evaluation to use to provide the specific feedback that could help the average preacher. "Nice sermon" is wonderful to hear, but what made it nice? What was working in the sermon that the preacher needs to know about and keep on doing? "I didn't care for that sermon, pastor" can be a hard thing for a preacher to hear. But it gets worse if the pastor asks, "Why?" only to hear the reply, "I don't know—I just didn't like it." Now the preacher has no idea what to do differently next time.

Suppose, then, those who listen to sermons want to be better sermon reviewers. What kind of vocabulary can we learn by which to articulate not just how we feel about a given sermon but also why? Maybe if we can find some evaluative pegs onto which to hang our post-sermon thoughts, both we and our preachers can gain a better understanding of what is, or is not, working in both a single sermon and the pattern of a certain pastor's preaching week to week.

What follows are four evaluation categories that my seminary has been using for a number of years to help people become more discerning sermon critics. By thinking along these lines, we may get better at diagnosing what makes some sermons sing and other sermons sink. What's more, if we are in a position in a congregation to help the pastor think through his or her sermons over time, these four categories may actually assist the preacher either to keep doing what is going well or to address what is going less well.

BIBLICAL

This category may seem obvious. Unless you attend a very liberal church or something like a Unitarian Universalist church (where the sermon is more likely to be based on Emerson or Thoreau than Luke or Romans), you expect that every sermon will be based on a Bible text. The text will be printed in the bulletin. Or it will appear on a screen. It will be read by the pastor or someone else just before the sermon begins. For most people, the words *sermon* and *Bible* go hand in hand.

As a category of sermon evaluation, however, pondering how or to what degree the sermon was biblical goes beyond its being somehow connected to a text that was read before the sermon. If we are honest, we have all heard sermons now and then that caused us to wonder in the end, "What did all of that have to do with Psalm 51?" Yes, the text for that week's sermon had been announced and read, but soon after the sermon began, the preacher went off in a direction that made the text recede. It was as though the text was something we can see in a car's rearview mirror that keeps getting smaller as we drive away from it.

Evaluating whether a sermon is biblical means being able to affirm whether the preacher said what he or she said because the sermon's key ideas, themes, and maybe imagery sprang straight from the Bible text to which the sermon was connected. If the text was Psalm 51, then the sermon talked about confession of sin and human sinfulness. If the sermon was based on the Cain and Abel story from Genesis 4, then the message talked about rivalry, giving in to envy, the tragedy of murder. If Romans 5 was the text, then the sermon centered on faith and how faith alone connects us to Jesus's saving work. In short, the focus of a given Bible passage will dictate the primary focus of the sermon.

But whether a sermon is biblical is more than even that. Did the preacher show evidence that he or she had spent the week really immersed in the text? As the preacher Roger Van Harn once suggested, preachers are kind of like scouts. They go out ahead of the congregation during the week to explore the territory of a given Bible passage. The preacher-scout may well discover far more treasures and curiosities than he or she has time to report on come Sunday, but the sermon will give the highlights. What's more, the preacher-scout will show some excitement about what was discovered. "I had a great time exploring these verses this week! Today I want to share with you the best of what I found!"

Most discerning listeners can tell if the preacher has done this exploratory work on behalf of the congregation. If in just reading the passage before the sermon, the preacher seems to trip over some of the words or reads somewhat haltingly, one might wonder just how much time the preacher spent inside those verses the last few days. The writer Gore Vidal once listened to a speech by President Dwight Eisenhower. Vidal wryly observed afterward that Eisenhower read his speech with a great sense of discovery. Preachers on Sunday had best not come off as being unfamiliar with their own chosen preaching texts!

One other hallmark of evaluating whether a sermon is biblical is determining whether the sermon did a thorough job uncovering at least some of the unique features of the Bible passage at hand. If it did, then the next time a person reads that passage, something from the sermon will come back to mind. "Oh yes. I remember that sermon on Mark 4. I remember the preacher mentioned that Jesus said he told parables so that people would *not* understand him. That is such a shock here! I remember the preacher pointing this out."

In most church traditions, pastors are ordained as ministers of the Word. That means it is their job to open up the Bible in their sermons. Sermons are not the occasion for preachers to talk primarily about other texts, other books. A sermon is not supposed to be a movie review or a time for the preacher to spout his or her own ideas on this or that subject. Yes, preachers need to apply God's Word, and perhaps different preachers will draw out different applications from the same Bible text. The point here, however, is that *what* gets applied comes right out of the Bible text at hand.

AUTHENTIC

Some years ago, after I began to teach at Calvin Seminary, I began to take guest preaching assignments at various local churches. One week after a service, an older woman came up to me to thank me for the sermon. She had really appreciated it. But then she said, "What I liked most was that I could tell you really believe all this stuff yourself."

Although I was glad to hear that, it made me wonder: How many sermons had she heard in which it was *not* clear the preacher was convicted by what he or she said? To what exactly did my sermon that day stand in contrast for her?

Of course, preaching should never be about the messenger first and foremost. Nor should the preacher constantly call attention to himself or herself. Still, a key to evaluating a sermon—a one-off sermon preached by a guest pastor or the one hundredth sermon we hear from our own pastor—is determining whether the messenger seemed authentic. Was it clear in listening to the preacher that his or her words were rooted in a life of real discipleship? Could we tell that the preacher knows what it is to struggle with certain parts of the faith? If there was something joyous and moving in the sermon, could we detect that it had moved the pastor's heart well before it moved everyone else's?

Conversely, did the preacher seem a bit detached from the sermon? Worse, did the pastor approach the text and the sermon with a kind of bored weariness? Did it seem that the preacher felt the sermon was just something to get through and so, virtually with gritted teeth, plodded on until it mercifully ended?

In his book *Blink*, Malcolm Gladwell made a startling assertion. Gladwell claimed that research has shown that most adults have a pretty keen intuition when it comes to sizing up people they meet. Within the first few seconds upon encountering someone for the first time, we make a number of snap judgments and assumptions as to what kind of person this is. Does she seem kind? Does he seem edgy? Is this someone we can trust or someone to be a bit wary around? Is this person angry or cynical? In under ten seconds, we form a welter of impressions in our minds, and, rather surprisingly, these snap assessments made in a blink very often turn out to be largely accurate. Even years later, after we have gotten to know someone pretty well, some of what we sized up during that first handshake turns out to be true.

People sitting in church have this kind of sixth sense when it comes to preachers too. We can tell pretty quickly if this pastor is eager to share this sermon. There is a bounce in her step, a twinkle in his eye, a fire in the belly that is palpable and contagious. Conversely, does the pastor seem bored? Or perhaps just tired? Can we tell if there is anything in this week's Bible text that sparked something in the preacher? Or is there a sense that the preacher thinks we have heard all this before so let's just get on with hearing it yet again? Blah, blah, blah.

To be clear, this is not a call for preachers to be hyperemotional every week. Authenticity should also certainly not be about a preacher trying to fake or force an enthusiasm that is not really there (even little kids are pretty good at sniffing out an adult who is faking it). "It seems like he was trying too hard," we might observe.

Some preachers, though, cannot hide their authenticity. Years ago in my denomination, there was a preacher—a good preacher by all reports—who was affectionately known by the nickname "Weeping Willie." In more sermons than not, before the message was finished, Pastor William would lose it and break down in genuine tears of joy, tears of contrition, tears of awe. Whatever the case, he cried a lot. None doubted how convicted this pastor was by the truths he proclaimed in his sermons. Most preachers do not cry that often, nor need they to count as authentic preachers. But however people perceive it, authenticity is a key category for sermon evaluations.

All through history, the best preachers have proclaimed God's Word out of a deep conviction in their own hearts that there is no message more beautiful than the gospel message. The preacher is one disciple of Jesus sharing the wonders of God's Word with fellow disciples. When that happens in genuine ways, listeners can tell. Authenticity is, then, a hallmark of what makes any given sermon a good sermon.

CONTEXTUAL

In chapter 2, we noted that history is filled with wonderful sermons written by people such as Augustine of Hippo and John Calvin. But we also noted that it would not work for someone in a church today to mount a pulpit and simply read such a sermon as it was originally written. The reason isn't just because old sermons contain words such as *behoove* and *foresooth*, which we don't generally use anymore. The main reason is because those old sermons were not written for our present context. Those messages were aimed at people from a different culture and time, with a different language and worldview. The issues of their day may or may not bear a resemblance to our current-day concerns. And even current-day concerns are very different in Uganda than in Cuba, in New Jersey as opposed to Manitoba. Yes, some things are timeless. Parents always worry about their children. People pray for peace and not war. The sin that too often clings to our hearts makes it difficult for us to bear the fruit of the Spirit, as the New Testament calls us to do. Still, the way we talk about such concerns varies from age to age, place to place.

Obviously, there are also things with which we struggle today—terrorism, the power of Hollywood movies, the temptations presented by the internet—that were not issues at all even a couple generations ago. Good preaching, then, will always be contextual. When we listen to a sermon, we should get the clear sense that the preacher is aware of our current time and place. Illustrations and references should display an accurate connection to where people live. Sermons given in Canada, for instance, ought not contain references to Congress, since in that setting, Parliament is the accurate political body to mention. Or if a pastor refers to mass media but talks about videotapes and record players in an age of digital streaming of movies and music, such a pastor is clearly out of step.

But contextuality involves more than such surface references. Sermons that are properly contextual display a deep pastoral awareness of people's doubts, fears, and questions. Some years ago, a friend of mine discovered a trove of old sermons from a Scottish preacher. The sermons seemed quite lively, very biblical, and well written. They seemed like really good sermons, until my friend realized they had all been written and preached in Britain during the darkest days of World War II. Yet not one sermon referred to the terror of German air raids. Not one sermon talked about the heartache of those who were worried about their sons on the front lines, much less those whose sons came home in coffins. Those sermons were "timeless" in the worst sense of the word. Similarly, in more recent years, can you imagine reading any sermons (in North America for sure) from late 2001 that did not mention, with some frequency, the horror of the 9/11 terrorist attacks?

Even concerns that might count as universal and have persisted throughout history have their own particular focus at any given moment. Parents have always been concerned for the well-being of their children, but today that concern might pass through the prism of fretting about human trafficking, internet predators, the specter of mass shootings at so many schools, racist comments and attacks, a spike in teenage suicides, and the too-easy availability of heroin.

With the internet and social media, the world is much smaller, and being contextual means being aware of issues even beyond the local church and community. Perhaps not every sermon needs to be a showcase of a given social issue of the day. But over time, sermons should clearly demonstrate that the preacher understands the twenty-first century, the current culture, the issues that keep people up at night. The Bible itself contains timeless truths. The content of the Bible and the God of the Bible are the same yesterday, today, and tomorrow. True. But the *context* into which that content comes is ever-changing. Good sermons will bring content and context together in ways that speak into people's lives in the present moment.

LIFE-CHANGING

We noted earlier that, biblically speaking, preaching as we now know it in the church has a long history. In some ways, it goes back to the prophetic office inaugurated by Moses. John the Baptist preached. So did Jesus. But the apostle Peter can still be credited with preaching the very first Christian sermon of the church. On Pentecost, after Peter wove together many biblical passages to show how they all were fulfilled in Jesus, the people in Jerusalem that day were thunderstruck. "What should we do?" they cried out. Peter told them to believe in Jesus and be baptized. Amazingly, three thousand people did. Right then and there. The church went from eleven former disciples and a few others to over three thousand in a day. That is the power of preaching!

Although most sermons have not come anywhere close to achieving that kind of dramatic conversion of masses of people, the ability to change lives still needs to count as an evaluation category for sermons. After all, the same Holy Spirit who was active in and through Peter's Pentecost sermon is still on the move through preaching in the church today. Everyone who preaches, therefore, and everyone who listens to sermons should, as theologian Neal Plantinga often notes, have the expectation that the sermon will be *eventful*. A sermon is never just about teaching or the distribution of information. Although deeply rooted in a biblical text, a sermon is never just a Bible commentary. Sermons should not be first of all pieces of entertainment or diversion. Sermons should be written, preached, and received with the up-front anticipation that the Spirit of God is going to *do* something.

Lives will change through preaching. Sometimes this change is as dramatic as a conversion from unbelief to faith. You never know when that might happen either. Years ago when I was the pastor of a church, a sixty-six-year-old man felt Jesus calling him after listening to a sermon I preached on the book of Jonah. This man somewhat randomly decided to visit our church, wandered in, heard a sermon on Jonah, and gave his life to Christ. Soon afterward, I baptized him. Jonah! Who knew?

But sermons can count as life-changing even short of full-scale conversion. Sometimes the Spirit will use a sermon to quicken the pulse of a longtime believer. Someone's faith will get a little deeper, seem a little more sure. A person might know that the end of life is a lot closer than it used to be but somehow through a sermon one week will feel more ready to face his or her own mortality and die into the arms of the Lord. Or a sermon will call someone back who had begun to wander. Faith had begun to seem a bit too fabulous, too hard to take seriously. But then the preacher said something that the Spirit winged into this person's heart, and, all of a sudden, faith seemed credible and true again.

Such changes of life need not be restricted to any one sermon. The Spirit also works through the arc of a given preacher's sermons week to week, month to month, even year to year. A life may be changed all at once through a single sermon, but a life can also be shaped, molded, and so changed over a long period of time. People who listen to sermons consistently should get to know the Bible better over time. They should find it easier to frame current events in a biblical-theological way. When a crisis hits someone's life, he or she should be able to draw from a built-up reservoir of strengthening and comforting truths heard over many years through the Word preached in church.

The Spirit of God is active and alive in preaching. The preacher should expect a sermon to make a life-changing difference. Those who listen should both sense and experience this very truth.

"How was the sermon?" Well, let's size it up. Was it deeply biblical? Did it come from an authentic messenger?

Was it preached into our current context? Was the Spirit at work to change lives in one way or another? If we can begin to answer these kinds of questions, we might just be able to provide preachers with the kind of sermon feedback that will genuinely help them in their holy task.

The Old
Story New

4

Some years ago when I was giving a lecture about preaching, the host for the event asked me, "If you could give only one piece of advice to any preacher, what would it be?" I thought for a bit before saying the only thing I could come up with in the moment. "Don't ever lose your ability to be surprised by the Bible." My answer was not particularly profound and may or may not be the best thing anyone could suggest to a preacher. But my host and those in attendance found it useful.

Many people who attend worship each week may eventually lose the sense that the Bible can surprise them. Perhaps in some church-plant settings or churches with many newer Christians, this is less true. But where people have been going to church for years, the Bible is familiar territory. Some have done the program "Read Through the Bible in One Year" multiple times. They have attended decades' worth of Bible study groups. They have heard thousands of sermons. True, some parts of the Bible are better known than others. Most know the story of Ruth pretty well, but the prophecy of Nahum not so much. The Gospel of Luke seems like an old friend, but the book of Ezra is more like a casual acquaintance. In and through it all, though, the Bible has few if any surprises left to disclose. Or so many people think.

Perhaps many preachers think this way too. If so, they may bring this overly familiar sense of biblical inevitability into the pulpit with them. We have read and heard these stories before—a million times, as we like to exaggerate. And so some preachers may think their job is just to keep retreading the same old, same old. Even studying the Bible becomes for some preachers the equivalent of a carpenter sawing a 2 x 4 board. A board's a board. You just keep cutting them the same way you've done countless times before. But this isn't true. At least for preachers it ought not to be true. And it ought not to be true for us listeners either.

We noted that the Bible and a specific passage of the Bible should form the core of every sermon. The less a sermon is tethered to a Bible text, the more it becomes something other than a true sermon. We also noted an old analogy that is often used regarding Scripture: it is like a pool. It is shallow enough for a toddler to splash around in safely yet deep enough to drown an elephant. In the context of the Christian church, sermons have been preached for two thousand years. At least 354 million new sermons are preached every year. Yet for all that, the Bible has not run dry. No one has said the church has run out of possible new sermons. Instead, the Holy Spirit keeps enlivening the biblical text and makes something new out of those ancient words every week.

If the existence of the Bible is itself a kind of miracle, then the seemingly inexhaustible riches of the Bible may be a miracle inside the miracle. Those who write sermons and those who listen to sermons should never think they have the Bible cased. We should never lose our expectation that something can yet surprise us right in the middle of even the most familiar Bible stories. In the rest of this chapter, I will suggest some things preachers and listeners can do to keep this expectation alive. But we will also ponder how and where we can locate ourselves inside the Bible's story.

THE GRAND STORY

A first thing to note is a point made by the outstanding preacher Thomas G. Long. Long once said that if you ask the average person, "What is the Bible?" you might hear something like the following: "The Bible is a book of doctrines and facts about God. The Bible is like an encyclopedia of divine concepts. Here and there—to help make things clearer—the Bible also throws in some stories to illustrate doctrines about God and creation and the like." But according to Long, that description is backward.

The truth is that the Bible is just one giant story. It is a singular narrative that stretches from Genesis to Revelation, from the dawn of creation to God's promise one day of a new creation. Contained within that single story are countless other, smaller stories. In the Bible, doctrines are not taught and then occasionally illustrated with stories. Instead, the Bible is a grand story, and all our doctrines and ideas about God emerge *from* the stories. Story is first. Divine concepts come second.

What the church has been proclaiming for a couple millennia now—and what Israel proclaimed even before the arrival of Jesus—is that the grand story is not just *a* story but *our* story. It is your story. It is my story. One way or another we are all characters in this divine drama. When I was a little kid, we read John 20 at the dinner table one night for devotions. In that passage, Jesus tells Thomas that he confessed Jesus as "my Lord and my God" because Jesus was standing right in front of him. Then Jesus said, "Because you have seen me, you have believed; blessed are those who have not seen and yet have believed" (v. 29). My mother then said, "Jesus means us. He's talking about us here." And I thought to myself, "Cool! I'm in the Bible!"

Some years later, when I got a little older and remembered thinking that, I felt a little foolish. Of course, I am not really in the Bible. But then I got a little older still. I even went to seminary. And eventually, I concluded I had been right in the first place: I am in the Bible. And so are you. So are we all. The Bible is a living story, not just a dry history of what once was. The Bible lives and breathes in a way no other book ever has or ever will.

OUR DAILY TROUBLES

In the sermons we hear, then, we can properly have the expectation that the preacher will help us see ourselves in the Bible's story. This needs to be true in two broad categories that I will borrow from the preaching scholar Paul

Scott Wilson and his book *The Four Pages of the Sermon*. Wilson claims that Scripture has a regular rhythm of presenting what he calls both trouble and grace.

By trouble, Wilson means the tension that comes whenever a sinful world (and a sinful people) encounter God and God's Word. The Bible was revealed to a fallen world precisely to address the situations that are common to all of us because of sin and evil. In the Bible, then, we find people getting themselves into a great deal of trouble. Cain murders his brother Abel. David commits adultery with a woman and arranges her husband's death to cover it up. The Israelites ignore God's Law and so abuse the poor and worship false gods such as Baal. Peter tries to be like Jesus in walking on water but instead begins to sink beneath the waves.

But there is a great deal of other trouble in the Bible too. Sometimes we doubt, as Sarah did when she laughed at God's promise that she would have a baby in her old age. Or we read the Psalms and agree with the pious poets who cry out, "How long, O Lord, how long? Will you ignore me forever? Where are you?" Or we hear Jesus telling us to love our enemies and to pray for those who are cruel to us, and we wonder, "Can anyone really do that?"

In many and varied ways, the Bible does a masterful job at displaying everything that troubles us in our lives. Questions, doubts, sinful mistakes, sickness, tragedy, natural disasters, idolatry, temptation—it's all in there. Ultimately, the Bible is not just the story of people from long ago and far away with names such as Solomon, Rahab, Jeremiah, and Miriam. The stories and the troubles of all those people have been preserved by God's Spirit so that we can see our own struggles reflected in the Bible. We can safely say that there is not a single instance of trouble in the Bible that is not right this very moment afflicting someone we know (or us). Preaching comes out of a very realistic book called Scripture. We should expect good sermons on this book to be as up-to-date as today's news headlines (or whatever we prayed about before going to church).

This means that sermons should talk about the things in life that trouble or bother us. The questions raised in sermons should be real questions that actual flesh-and-blood people of the twenty-first century care about. In what is now a widely quoted line, the preacher Harry Emerson Fosdick once said, "No one ever comes to church with a burning desire to answer the question, 'Whatever happened to the Jebusites?'" Yet we have all heard sermons that seem premised on the idea that we really did come to church for a history lesson. Or we came with intense curiosity as to what position Pontius Pilate occupied within the Roman governmental structure. At least that is what the preacher talked the most about in the sermon. "The preacher seems to think I am interested in this," we may think, "so maybe I should try to be."

Far better are sermons that target the real human issues in a biblical text and discuss them in light of our world now. We should expect when listening to sermons that on a fairly regular basis we will prick up our ears, sit up a little straighter, and say, "Hey, that question the preacher just mentioned is *my* question. When I can't sleep at 2:34 a.m. and I watch the bedside clock go to 3:25 and 4:15, that is the question that keeps me awake. I am listening now, pastor!"

THE BALM OF GRACE

But, of course, such intent listening to a discussion about trouble is only half of the equation. The other half is listening for what God's Word has to say regarding our doubts, our questions, our fears, our situations. This is the other big message of the Bible, or what Paul Scott Wilson calls grace. Yes, God's revealed Word is constantly intersecting with a fallen, sinful world. Troubles and tensions, questions and issues inevitably crop up at those intersections. But in those same passages, God does something, says something, promises something in ways that provide hope and comfort. Throughout the Bible, God—Father, Son, and Holy Spirit—is active and on the move. God's grace crashes into our world and into our lives in ways that bring healing and hope. To find grace in a text, we ask, "What is God doing in or through or behind this passage?"

Sermons should conclude with that kind of hope and should bring joy and at least some measure of relief to people who came into church weighed down by the burdens of life. Here, though, we run into a tension in the current church when it comes to preaching. It seems that in recent years, in an effort to be practical, some preachers have moved from proclaiming Good News to dispensing what could be called Good Advice. There are many how-to sermons these days. Sometimes the titles of sermon series reveal this trend: "Six Ways to Raise Successful Children," "Four Ways to Grow Your Marriage," "Five Ways to Make Your Dreams Come True." As some have observed, today some preachers sound less like Billy Graham and more like Dr. Phil. A hallmark of such DIY (do-it-yourself) preaching is ending the sermon with a to-do list.

For many people, such preaching puts the burden of responsibility to be better Christians squarely on already burdened shoulders. The sermon's final focus is less on God's active grace and more on how we need to get active to make God like us more or build the kingdom on our own or just generally take the initiative. Now, it is true there is such a thing as discipleship. We are called to bear the fruit of the Spirit. We are sanctified by the Spirit to lead holy, moral lives. And good preaching needs to encourage believers to do such things. But that kind of sacred living needs to happen inside the joyous Good News of grace! God through Christ and by his Holy Spirit has reconciled us freely and completely. We don't need to make God love us; he already does. He loved us even while we were yet sinners! This message of grace needs to shine through every sermon. We can never be reminded of this too much.

What's more, we need to let the Bible reveal to us all those instances of grace that form God's answer to our many troubles. The Bible never presents trouble without proclaiming or depicting God's corresponding good word that consoles us when we feel abandoned by God, as so many psalmists did. Sermons based on the Bible show us how God lifts us up when we sink into doubt, the way Jesus pulled Peter up out of the waves. The Bible shows us how God was compassionate even when Sarah laughed in the face of God's promises, and God is still kind to us when we, too, laugh as we wonder, "Will God really be able to make all things new?"

The God of the Bible does not tell us to go out and find our own solutions to whatever counts as trouble for us at any given moment. Instead, the Bible shows us a God who is on the move. Sermons that reflect the richness of Scripture gracefully throw us right into the middle of all that divine activity, as we get to go along for the ride of all that God is accomplishing. In this way, the old, old story of the Bible is really ever new and fresh because God did not stop acting and intervening and helping once the Bible was finished being written. If sermons make it sound as if God helped only all those people way back when, then we miss the freshness of a Word of grace today that produces hope and joy in our hearts.

SLOWING DOWN

I said at the start of this chapter that we need to keep alive the idea that the Bible can still surprise us. Every time we see this ancient Word coming straight into our present world and all its troubles, we are startled at what a living Word Scripture really is. No wonder the church has never run out of sermons! No wonder hundreds of millions of sermons a year never exhaust the Bible's riches! As long as we can see our lives reflected in the Bible—in both trouble and grace—that Word remains alive in us and in our pulpits and in our worship services every week.

Before we close this chapter, though, I want to share a practice that can make us more open to the Bible's surprises. This is a practice I share with seminary students, practicing preachers, and anyone interested in Bible study. My suggestion ties in with how we read the Bible. Too often—especially with familiar passages—we read the Bible in predictable ways. Suppose you sent twenty people off with a copy of the Luke 2 Christmas story. Suppose you asked them to record themselves reading the story aloud. Then suppose you collected the twenty recordings and hit play on each one at the same time. The odds are very good that each recording would slow down, speed up, and pause at the same places. We have heard these verses read so often that we all tend to read them the same way. Similar things would probably happen with recordings of Psalm 23 or Romans 8.

A key way to open ourselves up to seeing new things in old passages, then, is to break these reading habits. We need to read passages slowly and aloud. Perhaps we can try to read at a ridiculously slow rate so every word and phrase can soak in. If we try this, we will, by the Holy Spirit, almost certainly encounter new things in even the most familiar of stories.

Let me give an example. Years ago, I was preparing to preach a sermon for Christmas. I had chosen Luke 2 (because there are not that many Christmas options in the Bible!). But in my study, I read Luke 2 out loud and slowly. I then came to this verse: "The shepherds returned, glorifying and praising God for all the things they had heard and seen, which were just as they had been told" (v. 20). Again, we all "know" how to read this verse. We all know that the punch of it starts with the word *glorifying*, and so we race over the first half of the sentence to emphasize the glorifying and praising part.

By reading it slowly, however, I came to a full stop at "the shepherds returned." I had never paused to ponder just that part. Yes, they returned. They returned to their tattered tents and smelly sleeping bags. They returned to their sheep. They went back to work, to their routines, to everything that had characterized their lives before angels had appeared in a night sky. They had been to the cradle of God's Christ but . . . then it was back to work.

Isn't that the same for all of us? We celebrate Christmas every year with all the joy we can muster. We try to be festive. We sing the old carols. We deck the halls and the sanctuary and our homes with greenery and glittering lights. We come to the Christ's manger again and then . . . it's over. And we return. We return to school, to the office, to all that is ordinary. This can feel like the trouble in the text.

But as was the case with the shepherds, our encounter with the Christ means we return changed people. The birth of the Messiah does not solve all our daily problems. It does not instantly transform the world into a place where we always get to see angels dancing among the stars. Sooner or later, we return. But we can do so glorifying and praising God! And this is the grace! Our workaday worlds don't need to change in ways no one could miss for the joy of God's Christ to ring out in our hearts. Here is a marvelous truth we can take home with us when Christmas—or any worship service—ends.

I noticed this surprisingly new angle in a very familiar story when I slowed down to let the Spirit do its work. The Bible surprised me. It should do the same for all preachers, for all who listen to preachers, for all who read God's Word. It is always new and surprising. Thanks be to God!

The Nimble
Spirit

The sermon didn't work. Having just listened to the sermon, that is what Rev. Fred Rogers thought to himself as he sat in a church pew one Sunday many years ago. The message simply never took flight. The things the preacher said were ordinary and vaguely obvious, and when the sermon was not a bit boring, it was confusing. Rogers (and yes, we are talking about Mister Rogers) was about to share a bit of this negative assessment with the woman sitting next to him, but when he turned toward her, he noticed tears streaming down her cheeks. The sermon had spoken to her on a deep, quite personal level. Naturally, Rogers did not say what he had planned to say, but the encounter did make him wonder what had just happened.

Anyone who has regularly listened to sermons has no doubt had an experience like this one. Preachers certainly also know about this, albeit from a slightly different angle, because with some frequency, people thank preachers for things they never said. The first time this happens, the preacher may be tempted to whip out the sermon manuscript and say, "Look, here's what I said this morning, and as you can see, I most certainly did not say what you heard!" But assuming that what the person heard was not something offensive or something contrary to the preacher's beliefs, sooner or later preachers learn to let such things slide, to just take the compliment for things they

77

did not utter. If someone heard something lovely, why try to talk them out of it?

Sometimes, though, a situation does not involve someone hearing something the preacher did not say. Instead, someone puts a spin on something, applies something that was said but in a way the preacher could never have guessed anyone would. Yet how the person interpreted the sermon rang true. It was spiritually right. Perhaps it provided a given person with the very divine direction he or she had long been looking for. The person who delivered the message just never saw it coming.

THE SPIRIT AT WORK

How does this happen? Some might try to put forward any number of psychological theories to explain this. People hear what they want to hear perhaps. Or they repress certain negative things in order to elevate in their minds more positive matters and so reshape a message accordingly. Certainly, we have all had enough conversations (or arguments) in which we ended up exclaiming, "You're not listening to me! I never said that! You are twisting my words and taking what I said out of context!" When this happens to us, it can be deeply frustrating.

But in the tradition of the church, the explanation for what happens during the average sermon is more straightforward and spiritual: it is the work of the Holy Spirit. Throughout this book, we have asserted that the Spirit likes to work through preaching. Sermons on Sundays are by no means the only tool the Spirit uses to work among God's people or to get God's truths across to the world. But from Pentecost forward, the Word preached has been one of the Spirit's more common means of communicating, convicting, converting, and comforting God's people (and appealing to those outside the Christian faith too).

When talking to seminary students or others about this, I have often tried to invoke an image to represent the Spirit's work in preaching. In one sense, it would be easy to picture it this way: the preacher delivers a single message, and it goes straight from the preacher's mouth to the entire congregation. Perhaps we could envision this as a single black arrow pointing from the preacher to the people. Everyone gets the same message as a result. It would be like someone at a buffet dinner announcing into a microphone, "The food is ready! Help yourselves." Everyone hears this and so gets in line to begin scooping potatoes and chicken onto their plates. There was just one message to hear, and everyone heard the same thing.

But when it comes to preaching, we need a different visual image. Picture instead that coming from the preacher's mouth is not a single black arrow but a multitude of colored threads. There is one thread for each person sitting in the congregation, and each thread has a different color or shade. Each thread goes into the heart of a single listener. All the threads have a common source, of course, and so although there are many threads, they all contain mostly the same message, but not quite the same message in every sense. Instead, the Holy Spirit brings the sermon's words into each person's heart just a little differently. Those differences, of course, stem from what the Spirit knows any given person needs to hear. Some people need to be deeply comforted by a given truth, while other people need to receive that same truth as a convicting word. Some need to be confirmed in the work they are already doing, even as others need to hear the same word as a calling to something new.

There is a sense in which the preacher has no control over this. Yes, while the preacher is composing the sermon, hopefully many multicolored threads come *into* his or her head as he or she reflects on pastoral encounters, the needs of the congregation. The Spirit uses this, of course, but does so much more. Once the sermon gets delivered, the Spirit takes over, and then there is no telling what will happen next. The Spirit was involved all along in the preparation of the sermon, but the point is that once the words are spoken, marvelous things may happen.

A MYSTERY

As this chapter's opening story about Fred Rogers shows, marvelous things can happen even through a sermon that some find weak, confusing, or boring. Preaching and the act of listening to preaching are deeply mysterious. Most preachers will confess that there are some weeks when they are pretty pleased with the sermon. It seemed to come together well. The illustrations are good, the words seem, if not eloquent, at least pretty fine. On weeks like this, the preacher may approach the preaching moment with a great deal of confidence. And then somehow the sermon falls flat. It is not that anyone hated the sermon. It just didn't quite take wing. People were appreciative over-all, but there is a palpable sense that the preacher liked the sermon a whole lot more ahead of time than the congregation did after the fact.

Then again, there are some weeks when the preacher will say that writing the sermon was like pulling teeth. No ideas flowed smoothly; no good illustrations came to mind. By the time Sunday rolled around, the preacher was only too glad to be rid of the sermon and preached the message in the hopes that people would forgive this weak offering and come back for something better (hopefully!) the following week. And then . . . people were moved. The Spirit spoke to them. A few went so far as to tell the preacher that it was one of the better sermons in a while and they were just so grateful.

When I served as a pastor for a dozen years in one congregation, I had a particularly close confidant who was a member of the church. We communicated pretty regularly during any given week via phone or email. Mostly, we just chatted about ordinary stuff, but when I was having a particularly tough week, this friend would know. He would know if unexpected and stressful things had popped up.

He would know if, for whatever the reason, I was really struggling to get my thoughts onto paper for that week's sermon. Again and again, he told me over the years that many of the sermons that came out of stressful weeks or that were hard to write were among my best. Some of those very same stubborn sermons spoke to people, were used by the Spirit to accomplish some pretty wonderful things in people's lives.

So there you have it. Sometimes preachers are confident about sermons that just kind of lie there, and other times preachers feel bad about sermons that soar. As we say about life's little mysteries, "Go figure!" Most sermons are probably somewhere in between those extremes. Not every week has that level of surprising outcome. But the Spirit really does move in mysterious ways.

DOES EXCELLENCE MATTER?

All of this begs a poignant question: If the Spirit can work through any sermon, even one that on the surface might seem less than stellar, how important is it that the preacher work so hard on sermons? Is striving for excellence even worthwhile? How important is it that those who listen to sermons be ready to evaluate them using the categories detailed in chapter 3? After all, we might run through those four evaluation categories (biblical, authentic, contextual, life-changing) for a certain sermon and determine that it fell short in some key areas. Yet it may well be that the Spirit used that same sermon to touch someone. So what difference does it make what we think of a sermon? What difference does it make if the preacher worked hard to meet certain standards? Maybe we should all settle for mediocrity and let the Spirit do the heavy lifting for us.

As in all of life and in many areas of endeavor, the answer to questions about such matters is on one level pretty clear. The fact that something good might come out of something that does not represent someone's best effort is no excuse not to put forward our best efforts. A doctor who is sloppy in diagnosis or in ordering appropriate medical tests might manage to heal someone now and again. But if you knew that Dr. Smith is sloppy, would you choose him for your physician? A chef who cuts corners on cleanliness and uses ingredients that are stale or rotten might still serve some good meals. But that is no reason to prefer the restaurant, much less for the chef to be satisfied with being so lax. If this is true in nonreligious settings, how much more so in Christ's church, where the Spirit gives gifts to help communicate the greatest message the world has ever heard? Surely, the seriousness and importance of preaching call for preachers to do their best.

Yes, the Holy Spirit can and does work through all kinds of sermons. This is a profoundly good thing, since most sermons on any given Sunday are not going to rise to the level of masterpiece. Still, those of us who listen to sermons have a right to hope and pray that the preacher is cooperating with the Holy Spirit by doing everything he or she can to be clear, to be biblical, to be compelling and authentic and contextual and all the other things we thought about in chapter 3. Faithful preachers stay attuned to where the Spirit is leading them even as they use their skills to the fullest measure to the glory of God.

Those of us who listen to and evaluate sermons are also right to be on the lookout for the formal sermon components that contribute to strong messages. This is especially true if our role in a congregation means we are required to support and evaluate the preacher. The same Holy Spirit who can make even weak sermons sing is also the one who calls us to help one another in the body of Christ to give God our best.

But for those of us who listen to preaching every week, the nimbleness of the Spirit in applying sermons in so many ways may well mean something else. At minimum, it means we must not discount or dismiss the fact that someone was blessed by a sermon that left others unmoved. If *every week* we listen to sermons that fall short on multiple levels, then this becomes a concern that may need to be shared with the leadership of a congregation. But most things being equal, we should not sniff at those who feel a certain sermon spoke to them just because it did not appear to speak to others.

Perhaps a certain preacher's style appeals to some more than others. If many are being blessed but others not, it may be that the preacher is not a good fit for a given segment of the congregation. How one deals with such a situation varies. Some might choose to try to get what they can out of a style of preaching they don't like. Others might decide moving on to a different congregation would be best. Still others might try to help the preacher understand that a variety in sermon format and style would bless more people over the long haul.

Hopefully, we will not often find ourselves in such an extreme situation that requires us to make tough decisions. But being aware of the mystery that preaching is may help us frame such situations more charitably. Accepting that the Spirit regularly does surprising things through sermons may even open us up to encountering more surprises when listening to preaching week after week. This is not a call to be stoic and to stay in a preaching situation that does not feed our souls on a regular basis. But it is a call to appreciate a larger mystery in ways that expand our horizons when it comes to what can happen through preaching.

LOVE'S CONTEXT

A friend of mine once observed that when she began to attend a new church, she found the pastor's sermons to be generally just okay. Yet she had this firm sense that almost everyone else in the congregation deemed them far better than that. They were decidedly more positive about what they heard and how they received it than was probably warranted from an objective point of view.

What accounted for this? She found out the answer by listening to people's testimonies. It turned out that this particular preacher was a very fine pastor. He had stood at so many hospital beds, visited so many funeral homes, counseled lovingly with so many people in crisis. This was the context in which most people heard this man's sermons. And by the Holy Spirit of God, those sermons found a way into their hearts that might not have happened had they heard just one sermon from this man when he was a guest preacher one week.

The nimble Holy Spirit works in preaching through this interconnected web of pastoral care and love too. This is something for which preachers and congregational members alike should be deeply grateful.

Sermons
on the Move

6

Not so long ago in the 1980s, rumors about the death of preaching were being whispered about. By the 1980s, television and its unique forms of entertainment/communication had become well established culturally. Video technology and soon also computer innovations were taking off at rocket speed. The way people liked to receive information had been transformed.

Soon churches—including the fastest-growing megachurches in various parts of the world—began introducing visual elements into preaching. Slides, movie clips, onstage dramas, and other spectacles were capturing people's attention on Sunday mornings in churches that had stripped away everything that smacked of "your parents' church" in order to be fresh and new.

People began to wonder if regular sermons delivered by just one person could compete with all that. Perhaps drama teams and fast-paced video clips produced by a congregation's media department would replace the lone voice of the preacher. Or at the very least, perhaps such media would supplement sermons in ways that would soon make preaching as the church had long known it obsolete.

But then a funny thing happened as the world moved into a new century. In a number of places, new congregations were planted and grew rapidly, sometimes attracting ten thousand people every Sunday. Although most such churches featured modern music and worship styles replete with praise bands, praise teams, and newer songs, many of them had one other very striking feature in common: preaching. By one person. What is more, many of the younger people who joined these megachurches left congregations in which a typical sermon might last twenty minutes. When they joined these new, fast-growing congregations, they happily sat through sermons that might last upward of fifty minutes. Pastor Rob Bell founded what turned into a huge church, and he kicked things off with a series of sermons from the Old Testament book of Leviticus, each sermon lasting a good forty-five minutes or more. And people loved it.

The rumors of preaching's demise were, to use a well-known phrase, greatly exaggerated. Today in most churches worldwide, preaching still happens every Sunday in ways that people from five hundred, one thousand, and fifteen hundred years ago would still recognize as the proclamation of the gospel. Yes, many preachers dress differently now. Open-collar shirts and blue jeans have replaced robes and stoles in some (but not all) places. And yes, visuals on screens and the occasional movie clip might be included in sermons in ways not seen before more recent history. Still, preaching has had a way of hanging in there.

But that has been true for a couple millennia now (even longer if we trace some form of preaching all the way back to Moses). Preaching persisted when the Christian faith was officially persecuted and when it became the official religion of the Roman Empire. Preaching persisted when Augustine proclaimed his messages in Northern Africa and when Patrick brought the gospel to Ireland. Preaching persisted after the invention of the printing press and was one of the first forms of communication many took advantage of when something called the radio was invented. Today preaching also persists in our digital age as the internet lets people see and hear sermons from a variety of preachers from around the globe.

People often wonder what will be next for preaching. Some still wonder if one day something might happen to replace the Sunday sermon altogether. But our pondering of preaching in this book has returned again and again to a singular claim: the Holy Spirit likes to work through the Word preached. That was true on Pentecost. It will be true the next time Sunday rolls around. As far as we can see, it will remain true until that day when, as Jeremiah prophesied, "'No longer will they teach their neighbor, or say to one another, "Know the LORD," because they will all know me, from the least of them to the greatest,' declares the LORD" (Jeremiah 31:34). As Habakkuk also said, the day of preaching and prophesying will end because eventually "the earth will be filled with the knowledge of the glory of the LORD as the waters cover the sea" (Habakkuk 2:14).

Until then, though, we will listen to sermons, because in preaching, the Spirit of God speaks, the Spirit convicts, the Spirit comforts. When this happens, the enduring Word of God comes alive again and again.

At a dark time in ancient Israel's history, the people and even the leaders of the people had fallen so far away from God that we are told in 1 Samuel 3, "The word of the LORD was rare" (v. 1b). But then the Word of God came to the young boy Samuel. When that happened, the boy's mentor, Eli, told him how to respond: "Speak, LORD, for your servant is listening" (1 Samuel 3:9b).

Every Sunday when preachers stand up and look out at their congregations, it remains our privilege to say in our hearts, "Speak, Lord, your servants are listening."

Notes

Series Editor's Foreword

7   *Midway along the journey of our life:* The opening verse of
    Dante Alighieri, *The Inferno*, trans. Mark Musa (Blooming-
    ton: Indiana University Press, 1995), 19.

8   **"We are always on the road":** From Calvin's thirty-fourth
    sermon on Deuteronomy (5:12–14), preached on June 20,
    1555 (*Ioannis Calvini Opera quae supersunt Omnia*, ed.
    Johann-Wilhelm Baum et al. [Brunsvigae: C. A. Schwetschke
    et Filium, 1883], 26.291), as quoted in Herman Selderhuis,
    John Calvin: A Pilgrim's Life (Downers Grove, IL: InterVarsity,
    2009), 34.

8   **"a gift of divine kindness":** From the last chapter of John
    Calvin, *Institutes of the Christian Religion, 1541 French
    Edition*, trans. Elsie Anne McKee (Grand Rapids: Eerdmans,
    2009), 704. Titled "Of the Christian Life," the entire chapter is
    a guide to wise and faithful living in this world.

Chapter 1

15 **The great preacher and theologian Jonathan Edwards:**
    Jonathan Edwards, *The Works of Jonathan Edwards,* vol. 2,
    The Religious Affections, ed. John E. Smith (New Haven: Yale
    University Press, 1959), 115.

Chapter 2

27 **By some estimates:** Richard N. Ostling, "The Facts and Stats on 33,000 Denominations," Associated Press, May 19, 2001, http://www.philvaz.com/apologetics/a106.htm.

28 **As we dive into this history:** A good bit of the historical information contained in this chapter comes from William H. Willimon and Richard Lischer, eds., *A Concise Encyclopedia of Preaching* (Louisville: John Knox Press, 1995), 184–227.

39 **This change came about:** Fred B. Craddock, *As One without Authority: Essays on Inductive Preaching* (Enid, OK: Phillips University Press, 1971). Several revised editions have subsequently appeared.

41 **King ended with celebration:** The full manuscript of Martin Luther King Jr.'s "I Have a Dream" speech/sermon is widely available online, including here: https://www. google.com/url?sa=t&rct=j&q=&esrc=s&source=web&c-d=1&ved=2ahUKEwiEjdnT-6veAhWQTt8KHbSN-DRIQFjAAegQICRAC&url=https%3A%2F%2Fwww. archives.gov%2Ffiles%2Fpress%2Fexhibits%2Fdream-speech. pdf&usg=AOvVaw0miurGSC3wAgo_NHedH3oh.

41 **Only in recent years has this form of preaching:** Frank A. Thomas, *Introduction to the Practice of African American Preaching* (Nashville: Abingdon Press, 2016).

41 **Cone replied by saying:** James Cone also made this point more extensively throughout his book *God of the Oppressed* (New York: Seabury Press, 1975).

Chapter 3

49 **As the preacher Roger Van Harn once suggested:** Roger E. Van Harn, *Pew Rights: For People Who Listen to Sermons* (Grand Rapids: Eerdmans, 1992), 27–28.

49 **Vidal wryly observed afterward:** Gore Vidal, "The Best Years of Our Lives," *New York Review of Books*, September 29, 1983, https://www.nybooks.com/articles/1983/09/29/the-best-years-of-our-lives/.

51 **In his book *Blink*: Malcolm Gladwell:** Malcolm Gladwell, *Blink: The Power of Thinking without Thinking* (New York: Little Brown & Company, 2005).

Chapter 4

65 **A first thing to note:** Thomas G. Long, *Preaching and the Literary Forms of the Bible* (Philadelphia: Fortress Press, 1989), 66–69.

66 **This needs to be true in two broad categories:** Paul Scott Wilson, *The Four Pages of the Sermon: A Guide to Biblical Preaching*, rev. ed. (Nashville: Abingdon Press, 2018).

68 **In what is now a widely quoted line:** Quoted in Van Harn, *Pew Rights*, 58.

Chapter 5

77 **The sermon didn't work:** Lisa Belcher-Hamilton, "The Gospel According to Fred: A Visit with Mr. Rogers," *Christian Century*, April 13, 1994.